Measuring Weather

by Lucy Morris

illustrated by John Carrozza

 HOUGHTON MIFFLIN   BOSTON

It is a snowy day.
I want to see how much snow
has fallen on the ground.

I can use a ruler.
There is a lot of snow!

It is a windy day.

I can measure the wind two ways.

I can see which way the wind blows.
I can see how hard the wind
blows, too.

It is a rainy day.

I can see how much rain has fallen
from the sky.

It is a hot day.

I can see how hot it is outside.

You can measure the weather too.
Try it at home or at school!